Daddy's Disease: Helping Children Understand Alcoholism

Book 1 of the Helping Children Understand Series

Second Edition   May 2014

Other books by Carolyn Hannan Bell:

Mommy's Disease: Helping Children Understand Alcoholism

Illustrations by PeiPei

This is a work of fiction. Names, characters, businesses, places, events and incidents are either the products of the author's imagination or used in a fictitious manner. Any resemblance to actual persons, living or dead, or actual events is purely coincidental.

IBSN 9781493536757

For my sister, Jacqui, whose wisdom and strength have guided this journey, and so many others.

To my dear family and friends who supported me through writing this book. Much gratitude to Mom and Pop, Jacqui, Will and Alex, and to Nava, Francie, Karen, and Christie. Thank you Peipei for your wonderful illustrations. And to my husband, Ron, for your unconditional love and friendship - thank you is not nearly enough.

Once upon a time a boy named Tommy lived in a nice home with his Mom and Dad and his dog, Murphy. There were family dinners, movie nights and monster hunts and all was well, until Daddy started to change. He fell asleep on the couch a lot, sometimes even on the floor. He didn't come home from work for dinner like he used to, and when he did, he was acting strangely. He talked funny and bumped into things. Mommy and Daddy started to argue, and sometimes they yelled at each other. Daddy didn't play with Tommy like he used to and didn't seem to want to spend time with him. Tommy didn't understand what he had done wrong.

Now Tommy's parents don't live together anymore. He lives with his Mom and his dog, Murphy. He misses his daddy a lot. Tommy and his daddy are supposed to see each other every week, but sometimes his daddy is busy and doesn't show up when he's supposed to.

It was six fifteen on a Tuesday evening, only fifteen minutes before Tommy's dad had promised to take him to their favorite Mexican restaurant. Tommy had been looking forward to this night for three whole days—just he and Daddy and as many tacos as they could eat! Sometimes fifteen minutes could seem like a month! Then fifteen minutes turned into twenty, and twenty turned into thirty, until it turned into time for Tommy to go to bed. His dad never came and Tommy didn't know why.

Murphy jumped right into bed with Tommy and tried his best to cheer him up with kisses and cuddles. But Tommy was too sad.

Mommy came into the room and sat on the edge of Tommy's bed and wiped his tears.

"Dad promised he'd be here. Why doesn't daddy want to be with me? Why doesn't he love me? What did I do wrong?" Tommy cried.

Mom held Tommy close and stroked his hair. "Daddy loves you very much. You didn't do anything at all to keep him from coming tonight."

Tommy buried his head under the covers and Murphy followed right in after him.

Mom peeked under the blanket at Tommy and gently explained, "What happened tonight didn't have anything to do with how much Daddy loves you. The reason he didn't come tonight is that he has a disease that makes him forget the things he promises you. It makes him act in ways that he's ashamed of."

"That's silly," said Tommy.

Murphy cocked his head and looked at Mommy as she explained.

"The disease is called alcoholism and a person who has the disease is called an alcoholic. Daddy is an alcoholic."

Tommy was too tired and too sad to talk anymore that night, so he cuddled up next to Murphy and went to sleep.

Something weird happened at school that week. Tommy's best friend, Ronnie, was home sick all week with chicken pox.

Miss Poughkeepsie, his teacher, explained to the class that chicken pox is a disease that causes itchy bumps and is really easy to catch.

Tommy missed Ronnie a lot and wished he would come back to school and play with him. Instead, he played with his other good buddies, Alex and Will. Together, they made a get well card to help Ronnie feel better.

As Tommy was walking home from school he started to think about what his Mom had said about his father's disease and he wondered if it was like Ronnie's disease. As soon as he got home, he told his mom about Ronnie's chicken pox.

"Ronnie has chicken pox and he had to stay home so the other kids wouldn't catch it. Is Daddy's disease like chicken pox?" asked Tommy.

"Well," answered Mommy, "There are some things that chicken pox and alcoholism have in common. The first thing is that it's nobody's fault when someone gets either disease.

Tommy nodded his head and said "Yeah, you can't help it if you get sick!"

"Right," answered Mom, "and when you have chicken pox your skin feels really itchy and it's very hard not to scratch. But if you scratch you could get some pretty icky scars, so you have to try really hard not to scratch."

"Does Daddy itch?" interrupted Tommy.

"No, Honey. Daddy doesn't have chicken pox, he has alcoholism. It's not itchy, but in the same way it's hard not to scratch an itchy chicken pox, it's really hard for Dad not to drink alcohol."

"So, Daddy has a disease that makes him really thirsty?"

Murphy licked his lips.

"Not exactly," explained Mommy. Tommy was getting confused. "Alcoholism makes Daddy's body have a kind of allergy to beer, wine and liquor which are all types of alcohol. When he drinks alcohol it's hard for him to stop and then the alcohol affects how he thinks, feels and behaves."

"It's kind of like your allergy. Do you remember what happens to you when you eat peanuts?" Tommy thought for a moment, and said, "Like the time when I ate that cookie with peanut butter in it and it made me not be able to breathe?"

"Exactly," said Mommy, "there isn't anything you can do to make yourself not be allergic to peanuts, right?"

"Yeah, so I just don't even eat peanuts 'cause I never want not to be able to breathe again!"

Murphy thumped his tail and licked Tommy's cheek.

"How come Daddy keeps drinking alcohol when it makes him act in bad ways? Why doesn't he stop drinking alcohol like I stopped eating peanuts?"

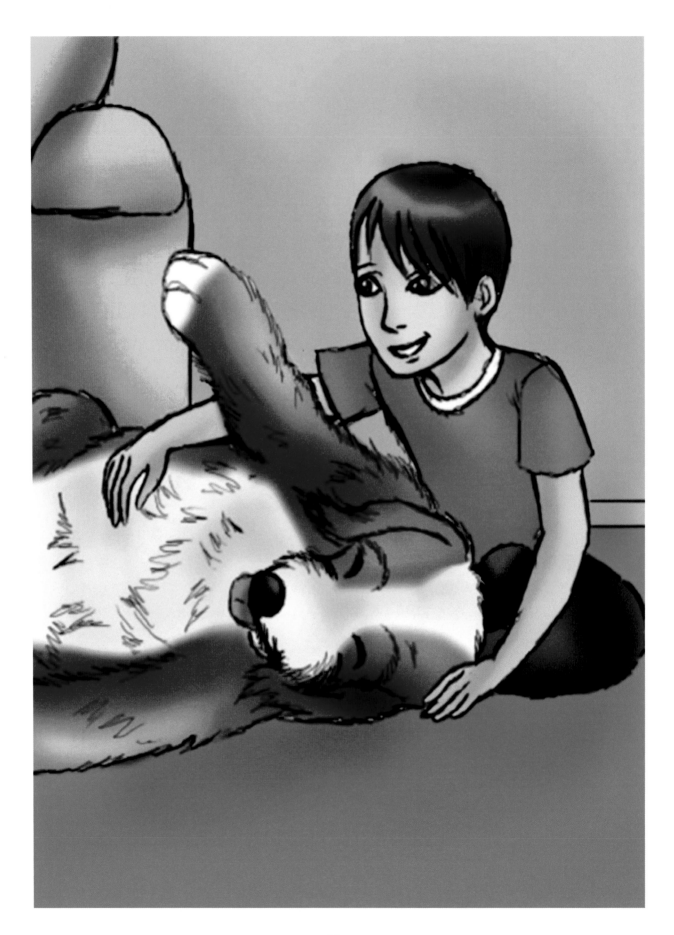

Mom thought for a bit and said slowly, "It's kind of difficult to explain. Daddy's disease makes him crave alcohol. That means that his body really feels like it wants alcohol. It's like a voice inside him that says `have a drink- it will taste sooooo good, and you will feel sooooo much better'".

"A voice inside his brain that tells him to do things?", Tommy questioned.

"Well, it can be a voice or a really strong feeling that nags at him all day and all night long and it doesn't stop until he takes a drink. Once he takes even one drink, it's very, very hard for him to stop drinking until he falls really deeply asleep."

Tommy felt confused and tried to understand what Mommy was saying. Finally, he looked up at her and said, "I don't understand that."

Murphy rolled over on his back so that Tommy would scratch his belly. He was getting pretty confused by all of this, too.

,

Tommy had enough of this conversation and wanted to talk about his Halloween costume and trick-or-treating. Halloween was only one week away!

He couldn't decide if he was going to be Spiderman, or maybe a Zombie, or a vampire, or a pirate, or....

Mommy said, "Why don't you think of your very favorite thing in the whole world and be that for Halloween?" Murphy nuzzled Tommy's hand in agreement. Tommy looked at Mommy with a huge grin on his face and said, "I'm gonna be Murphy for Halloween!!!!"

It was the best Halloween ever! Ronnie's Chicken Pox was all gone, so Tommy went trick-or-treating with him, and Will and Alex. They stayed out for hours going from house to house and collecting more candy and goodies than they ever thought possible! Tommy couldn't wait to get home and dump his treats on the kitchen table and dig in!!

When he got home it was really late—almost eight o'clock at night. Mommy said that Tommy could have two small pieces of candy before he got ready for bed. Tommy felt very disappointed. "Two? Come on, Mom! Puleeze, puleeze can I have just four, puleeze?" Murphy thumped his tail in agreement.

"Candy will make it harder for you to get to sleep. Two is plenty and you can have more tomorrow." Mommy sounded really serious, so Tommy ate his two pieces (it was really hard to pick just two) and got ready for bed.

After Mommy tucked Tommy and Murphy into bed, they both felt restless and excited. They were thinking about how much fun they had trick-or-treating, but mostly they were thinking about all that delicious candy only a few steps away in the kitchen. They tossed and turned and tried really hard to squeeze their eyes closed, but it wasn't working. All they could think about was CANDY!!!

So, Tommy and Murphy quietly slid out of bed and crept across the floor and down the stairs to the kitchen. They were very careful not to wake Mommy as they snuck past her bedroom door. They knew how upset she would be if she caught them, but they didn't seem to be able to help themselves.

Finally, they got to the kitchen and pulled the giant pillow case filled with candy onto the floor and dug in. The chocolate and caramel and sweet and sour and soft and chewy and crunchy tastes were so yummy that they didn't think of anything else other than how good they felt. They didn't even hear Mommy come into the kitchen.

Mommy was not happy. Tommy's face was smeared with chocolate and Murphy's beard had sticky, gooey caramel stuck in it. Tommy knew he was in big trouble, but the worst part was that Mommy didn't even yell at him. She just looked so sad and told Tommy how disappointed in him she was, which made him feel sad and ashamed.

He didn't like that feeling at all.

Mommy cleaned up their faces, and made Tommy brush his teeth for a really, really long time.

Then she put them both back in bed, turned out the light and closed the door. Tommy felt just terrible about what he'd done.

 And also kind of sick…

When Tommy woke up the next morning he could hear Mommy making breakfast in the kitchen. The thought of food made his stomach feel funny.

He was so sorry he had not listened to Mommy and had eaten all that candy. He felt awful, but it was a school day and Tommy had to go.

Plus, a policeman was coming to school to give a special talk that he had been looking forward to for weeks!

After he dressed, he and Murphy went downstairs—hoping that Mommy wasn't still mad at them. "Good morning, you two. How are you feeling, today?" Mommy asked.

Tommy didn't want to tell her the truth because he knew that it was his own fault that he felt sick. "Okay," he said, but he really wasn't.

When he saw the waffles waiting for him at the table his stomach hurt and his face turned green. Mom sent him back to bed.

He was going to have to miss school, the policeman and his friends, and it was his own fault.

Tommy was so sad and disappointed that he couldn't sleep. After a while Mom came in and sat on the edge of his bed, felt his forehead, and gave him a kiss.

Tommy cried, "I'm so sorry I hurt your feelings by not doing what you told me."

Mommy answered, "This has nothing to do with my feelings. You weren't thinking about me when you ate that candy. But, maybe you can use this experience to understand Daddy's disease a little better."

"Huh?" asked Tommy. Murphy cocked his head.

"Well, you didn't eat that candy because you didn't love me enough, or because I wasn't being a good enough Mom—just like Daddy doesn't drink because he doesn't love you enough, or think you aren't being a good enough son!"

Mom pulled Tommy close to her and explained, "You know how impossible it was for you to have a whole pillow case filled with candy and only have one or two pieces? Remember how it felt like one, or two or even three pieces were not enough! And how that voice in your mind kept telling you how good another piece of candy would taste? Remember how hard it was to think about anything else?

"Well, that's kind of what it's like for Daddy or anyone else who has a drinking problem. The difference is that the voice inside Daddy's mind is there all the time—every day and every night. That's what makes it so hard for him not to have a drink. Once he starts drinking, it's even harder for him to stop."

"I remember. But, I'm never gonna eat too much candy again. I feel so sick and I missed the policeman at school!! Maybe we should tell Daddy that he will feel sick from alcohol if he has more than one drink?"

"Daddy already knows that. He's the only one who can stop his drinking. He knows that he should stop. He knows that drinking will make him feel sick and make him miss things, but it's just so hard to stop once he starts. That's the disease part of alcoholism," explained Mommy. "An alcoholic can't stop after one or two or even seven drinks. Once he has one drink he'll usually keep drinking until he falls asleep."

"So Daddy could just never drink again and then he won't be an alcoholic anymore!" exclaimed Tommy.

Mom smoothed Tommy's sheets where Murphy rumpled them and said, "No, alcoholism never goes away. But, an alcoholic can make the choice to stop drinking alcohol. There are special people who can help him learn how to stop. That's called 'being in recovery.'"

"So that means that Daddy can never have a drink again? Not even one? Not ever?"

"That's exactly right, sweetie," said Mommy. Tommy hugged Murphy close and thought about all the things Mom was teaching him.

"So how come the alcohol makes him forget stuff and act mean sometimes?" asked Tommy.

Mommy held Tommy's hand and explained, "Alcohol affects your brain and makes you say or do things that you wouldn't normally do. It's a little bit like how you get when you're really sleepy or really hungry. You get grumpy and tired and it's hard for you to behave well. "

After a few moments Tommy looked up at Mom and said angrily, "If Daddy really loved me then he would never drink alcohol at all. He wouldn't drink things that make him say mean things, or yell or forget to take me places. If he loved me…"

"Whoa! Whoa!" Mommy interrupted. "Daddy's drinking doesn't have a thing to do with you, or me or anyone or anything. He drinks because he chooses to drink, because of that voice inside his mind and because he hasn't learned how not to drink."

Tommy's eyes filled with tears as he said, "If Daddy loved me then he just wouldn't have any drinks at all!"

"Did you eat all that candy because you didn't love me?" asked Mommy. "Of course not, it's the same thing with Daddy's drinking."

Murphy seemed to agree and began to chew on this favorite stuffed kangaroo.

Mommy hugged Tommy tightly and kissed the top of his head.

"Your Daddy loves you more than anything in this whole world," she said. "It's this terrible disease, and nothing else that makes him drink and it's the drinking that makes him behave badly. None of this has anything to do with you!"

"Do you remember all the ways your Dad has shown you how much he loves you? Like when he helped you build that race car for Cub Scouts, and took you camping, and taught you to ride your bike?"

Tommy's eyes lit up, "Like when he took me fishing on his bass boat with Murphy and we caught seven giant fish?!!!!"

Tommy drifted to sleep with dreams of all the fun things he and Daddy had done together and how good he felt thinking of those fun times.

When Tommy got up the next day, he realized it was Saturday and he could spend the morning watching cartoons and wrestling with Murphy. He still felt tired from all the talking he and Mom did the night before. Talking about hard things, like Daddy's disease, took a lot of energy! He had to rest up for his afternoon play date with Ronnie.

But, things didn't go so well with Ronnie this time. Ronnie really wanted to ride bikes and Tommy really wanted to play video games and they got into a fight. Tommy was too tired and too upset to work things out with Ronnie, so he called his Mom to come and pick him up early.

On the way home, Mom wanted to know what happened, but Tommy didn't want to talk about it. Mommy reminded him how important it is to talk about feelings, especially hard feelings. Tommy exclaimed, "Ronnie wouldn't do what I wanted and I was his guest!" Mom thought for a moment and asked, "Did you try and work things out with him? Did you look for a compromise so you could both be happy?" "No," answered Tommy, "I didn't feel like talking to him. I was too mad!"

When they got home Mom let Tommy play video games and calm down a bit. Then she came over to him on the couch and told him that they needed to talk a bit about how important it is to work problems out. She told him that not talking about hard things is something that Daddy has trouble with too.

"I think that what happened today may help you understand Daddy's disease a bit more," said Mom. Murphy looked up from his kangaroo to hear what she had to say. "Daddy drinks alcohol because it helps him to not think about his problems. It makes him forget about the hard or painful things in his life like difficulties at work or arguments he might be having with me. Unfortunately, it also makes him forget about the good and loving things in his life like you and the fun things that you and he do together. That's why Daddy often breaks his promises to you—the alcohol makes him forget that he ever made the promises in the first place!"

"You always tell me to talk about my problems." Tommy said proudly.

Mommy put her arm around Tommy and said, "That's a really good way to work on the things that are bothering you. But, drinking and forgetting is Daddy's way of handling his problems. So, not only does the voice inside his mind tell him that he should drink, he drinks because it's the only way he really knows how to make his troubles and bad feelings go away."

"You mean if Daddy is sad or mad at something, he thinks that if he drinks some alcohol then he won't feel sad or mad anymore?" asked Tommy.

"That's right," answered Mom, "but, when he wakes up after being drunk, his problems will still be there. Then he'll still feel sad and mad and also ashamed for having gotten drunk again."

Tommy looked up at Mom, "You mean that Daddy feels ashamed of drinking? What's 'drunk'?"

"'Drunk' is what happens to your body after you drink too much alcohol," said Mommy, "and yes, Daddy is very much ashamed when he gets drunk.

He doesn't want to disappoint you or to let you down. Each time he does, he feels worse about himself. But, he doesn't know any other way to deal with those feelings other than to try and make them go away with more drinking. It's a circle that just keeps spinning around."

Murphy and Tommy both groaned.

"Does that mean that he could still love me and be mean to me at the same time? He could love me and not show up at my soccer game, or take me to dinner?"

"That's exactly right", Mommy answered. "He acts the way he does because of his drinking and never, ever because of his feelings for you. He drinks because he is sad and he is sad because he drinks."

"What if I were really, really good and didn't cause any problems? What if I never asked Daddy to take me anywhere, and did all of my homework and cleaned my room? Then he wouldn't feel so sad or have any more problems and then he wouldn't have to drink!"

Mom took Tommy's hand and said, "Oh Honey, you have to try to understand that Daddy doesn't drink because of anything you do or anything you don't do. He drinks because he has a disease and because he hasn't figured out a way to not drink. He loves you with all of his heart and he always will. There isn't anything that you could do, good or bad, that would, in any way, cause Daddy to drink."

"How could he figure out not to drink?" asked Tommy.

"First," said Mommy, "Daddy has to want to stop drinking. He has to admit to himself that he has a problem and that he needs help to solve it. After that, there are really helpful groups like Alcoholics Anonymous that he could join. There are people there who could teach him ways to handle his problems and his feelings without drinking alcohol."

"Can we take him there? Maybe tomorrow?" asked Tommy. Murphy's tail thumped loudly on the bed.

"No, Honey. That's something Daddy has to do on his own. We didn't cause his drinking problem and we can't fix it. You can support him and cheer him on if he decides to get better, but until then, you have to protect your feelings."

"Protect my feelings from what?"

"Well," said Mommy, "it's not good for you to believe that you can make Daddy drink or not drink. When you think that Daddy drinks because he doesn't love you enough to stop drinking, or that something you did caused him to drink—that's the same as thinking that everything he feels and does is because of you. That's simply not true. He loves you and he always will no matter what. You just have to remember that Daddy is in charge of himself. You can only be in charge of you."

"But, if I never did anything bad wouldn't that make it easier for Dad to not drink?" asked Tommy.

"One has nothing to do with the other. Even if everything were the best it could possibly be Daddy would still drink. It isn't about what's going on around him—he drinks because of what's going on inside of him. He doesn't know how not to drink and nothing and no one can change that except him." Mommy explained.

"So what should I do?" asked Tommy.

Mom put her arms around Tommy and said, "You just keep being the wonderful, sweet little boy you are. Don't change a thing about yourself. Your job is to do your best to grow and to learn. That's what all of us are here to do!

Daddy will find his own way. All we can do is hope that he'll find a way that doesn't include alcohol. You just keep being the best you that you can be, and keep trying to understand that Daddy makes his own choices and that those choices aren't because of anything you do or don't do. He loves you with his whole heart, just like I do."

Murphy licked Mommy right on the nose and Tommy giggled.

"Daddy's disease may cause him to act like that's not true, but that's where you may have to work the hardest—to keep thinking about what you've learned about alcoholism. You have to work extra hard to remember that alcohol, and not you, is what makes Daddy behave badly. The way Daddy acts is not your fault."

Murphy snuggled up onto Tommy's pillow. His favorite place to sleep was right next to Tommy's face.

Tommy leaned back on his pillow and closed his eyes. "I think I can sleep now, Mom. I hope Daddy's okay, but I'm glad that he's not mad at me." Mom gave Tommy a kiss on the forehead and pulled his covers up snuggly to his chin. "Goodnight, sweet boy", she said "We'll keep talking about this and figuring things out as we go and all will be well. I love you so much, always will, never won't."

And, she turned out the light to welcome Tommy's sweet dreams.

Carolyn Hannan Bell is a practicing Psychotherapist in New Jersey. She works with families and individuals suffering from the emotional effects of alcohol and substance abuse. This is her first children's book.

PRAISE FOR DADDY'S DISEASE

"Absolutely wonderful. I have counseled so many kids
who would have benefitted from this book."
Gail McVey, Psy.D., School Psychologist

"This is an important book in that it brings the shame and secrecy of alcoholism into an arena of understanding for children who often feel responsible for the actions of their parents. It is an excellent addition to this library's collection."
Karen Casaceli, M.Ed., M.L.I.S. School Library Media Specialist

"Carolyn's words in this book will gently encourage difficult conversations to begin while allowing the little one not to feel alone or unloved... what a powerful, transformative gift awaits the reader of this book. I highly recommend it."
Frances Schwabenland, M.S., M.Ed.

"The author clearly understands the mind of an alcoholic, and does a fine job explaining it in a simple, easy to understand manner. I was most surprised to find that the book, while geared towards children, explains alcoholism so simply yet so well that I find myself wishing that many adults in my life could read and grasp the message that this short book drives home. It is, in my opinion, a great read for anyone that has someone suffering from alcoholism in their lives." Keith W.

"Daddy's Disease is a well written and informative book that manages to connect with kids of all ages. It addresses the feelings that so many kids of alcoholic parents have and helps them understand those feelings as well as understand alcoholism. I was impressed with how well the author was able to explain the disease of alcoholism in terms that a child can relate to. This book will help so many children deal with their feelings of hurt and confusion. A MUST read!" Suzanne K.

"This is a "spot on" book for children of alcoholics. I had a Daddy Disease, so you can relate. More people than not need to read this book." Maddie L.

"Carolyn Hannan Bell has captured the heart of children in a way that few can. Her insight to a child's confusion when living with alcoholism is incredibly valuable as she touches on issues that many adults fear to tread. Carolyn's ability to see into the heart of a child is nothing less than phenomenal. This is the most effective tool I have ever read when dealing with children and their understanding of alcoholism."
Monty Dale Meyer, CEO, Take 12 Recovery Radio * KHLT Recovery Broadcasting

"We love and miss you, Murphy."

Carolyn's webpage: www.alcoholismhurtskids.com

Made in the USA
Middletown, DE
27 January 2020